1 2

FOR YOU AND ME

by

MERIDA WOODFORD

1 hot air balloon

one

2 **toy cars**

two

3 juggling balls

three

4 milking cows

four

5 happy squirrels

five

6 huge sunflowers

six

7 shiny beads

seven

8 new buttons

eight

9 birthday candles

nine

10 floppy hats

ten

11

hen's eggs

eleven

12 fluffy clouds

twelve

13 singing birds

thirteen

14 drying socks

fourteen

15 bright butterflies

fifteen

16 yellow ducklings

sixteen

17 dinner plates

seventeen

18 flying kites

eighteen

19 red roses

TO YOU xx

nineteen

20 Christmas bells

twenty

21 buzzing bees

twenty-one

22 sailing boats

The Adventurer

twenty-two

23 rosy apples

twenty-three

24 woolly sheep

twenty-four

25 glowing stars

twenty-five

At the village fête can you see:-

1 hot air balloon   3 juggling balls

2 toy cars   4 milking cows

5 happy squirrels   8 new buttons

6 huge sunflowers   9 birthday candles

7 shiny beads   10 floppy hats?

How many elephants are there fast asleep?

How many squirrels are there climbing up the ladder?

How many tired animals are there going home to bed?

Printed in England. ISBN 085503 178 6